ID030432

WRITING AND CRITICISM

A Book for Margery Bianco

WRITING
AND
CRITICISM

A BOOK FOR MARGERY BIANCO

Edited by
ANNE CARROLL MOORE AND BERTHA MAHONY MILLER
DECORATED BY VALENTI ANGELO

THE HORN BOOK, INC. BOSTON 1951

INTRODUCTION

NOT yet is it generally understood, much less has it been said in print, all that books may afford to children in the nourishment of heart and soul. Margery Bianco made a rich contribution to this understanding in her own books and in all that she wrote in reviews or other critical essays.

As last work was being done on this introduction, I read William Faulkner's words spoken on the occasion of the award to him of the Nobel Prize in Literature in Stockholm, December 10, 1950. His short address included the following paragraphs:*

"He [the young man or woman writing today] must teach himself that the basest of all things is to be afraid; and, teaching himself that, forget it forever, leaving no room in his workshop for anything but the old verities and truths of the heart, the old universal truths lacking which any story is ephemeral and doomed — love and honor and pity and pride and compassion and sacrifice. . . .

I decline to accept the end of man . . . I believe that man will not merely endure; he will prevail. He is immortal, not because he alone among creatures has an inexhaustible voice but because he has a soul, a spirit capable of compassion and sacrifice and endurance. The poet's, the writer's, duty is to

* See page 93 for Acknowledgments.

write about these things. It is his privilege to help man endure by lifting his heart, by reminding him of the courage and honor and hope and pride and compassion and pity and sacrifice which have been the glory of the past. The poet's voice need not merely be the record of man, it can be one of the props, the pillars to help him to endure and prevail."

During hours upon hours of newspaper reading in a period of tremendous national and international stress and strain these were the bravest words I had read. It was particularly cheering to have them come from a writer of literature.

They embodied, too, the spirit of the life and work of the bravest person I have been privileged to know. We have shaped this book to make something of Margery Williams Bianco's life and work known to later generations.

Margery Bianco wrote nineteen books for children and young people. Her novels, a book on gardens, a book on Paris and translations from the French bring the number of her published volumes to twenty-seven. On September 4, 1944, after an illness of three days, Margery Bianco died and an important creative writer for children and young people and a rarely able critic passed out of the field of children's books.

Margery Williams was born in London on July 22, 1881. Her father was a barrister and a distinguished classical scholar. Her earliest recollections were of walks along the Thames Embankment and in the Chelsea Pensioners' Gardens where the nice old veterans of the Crimean War would cut her big bunches of mixed flowers from their garden plots. Since her sister was six years older, Margery played much by herself and made up her own games, the favorite being to trace and cut out the animals pictured in her NATURAL HISTORY and so have her own zoo. These paper animals were later superseded by pet mice who took possession of the big doll house and brought up their families there.

She paid her first visit to America when she was nine years old and spent most of her outdoor time that summer in Central Park, then quite wild, where besides the zoo and the donkeys and the merry-go-round there were all kinds of birds and butterflies and strange insects she had read of but never seen. After New York she lived on a farm in Pennsylvania and experienced all the country doings she had read about in ST. NICHOLAS back in England — berry-picking, corn-husking, coasting in winter and long drives about the countryside with a horse and buggy. After a year in the country she went at last to a day school in Philadelphia, with an occasional year or so back in England but no school there. Then two happy years in the Convent School at Sharon Hill, Philadelphia — the years from fifteen to seventeen — gave her the longest consecutive schooling, and the last, she ever had. The next few years were spent backward and forward between England and America. At seventeen she began to write and her first novel was published in England in 1902.

In 1904 Margery Williams married Francesco Bianco. A graduate of the University of Turin, Francesco Bianco had come over to London while quite a young man, with a deep and instinctive love and appreciation of books and the fine arts. There he began at once to build up his knowledge of rare books and worked for a time for the firm of Zaehnsdorf, book dealers, before he became manager of the rare book department of Brentano's in Paris. A few years after Francesco Bianco's arrival in London, he sent for his younger brother, Angelo, and arranged for him to attend an English boarding school. This is the Uncle Angelo of whom Pamela writes in Chapter II. Captain Bianco died in New York on July 21, 1946.

For three years after their marriage the Biancos lived in London. There Cecco was born on August 15, 1905, and Pamela, sixteen months later on December 31, 1906. When Pamela was six months old they went to Paris, returning to London in 1911 for a stay of three years. These three years so far as she and Cecco were concerned, Pamela has described in her book PARADISE SQUARE, published in the fall of 1950. In 1914 the Biancos settled in Italy at Turin and spent the four years of the First World War there. Francesco Bianco was called early to service in the Italian Army and became a captain.

Pamela had been drawing from her earliest years and when in 1919 her family returned once more to England her drawings were shown at the Leicester Galleries in London. Out of that exhibition came the book FLORA and those "illustrative poems" which the drawings inspired Walter de la Mare to write. In 1921 Captain Bianco and Pamela came over to New York for the exhibition of Pamela's work at the Anderson Galleries, and soon afterward Margery came with Cecco.

Cecco attended the Donaldson School for boys in Ilchester, Maryland, for two years and then went to Columbia University. Upon the completion of his studies there, he joined the staff of the Anderson Galleries where he spent a long time working in the rare book department and doing research and evaluation work upon the books preceding the auction sales, staying on after the Galleries became the American Art Association-Anderson Galleries. Cecco has always had, like his father, a natural interest in books and the fine arts, and learned a great deal about rare books from his father. During World War II Cecco held a government post in Washington. In 1947 he went to Frankfort, Germany, to work for the United States Military Government, his wife (formerly Jean Wallace) following a year later with their two children, Michael and Brenda.

After 1921 we were fortunate to have this talented family living and working in this country for, as Louise Seaman wrote in THE HORN BOOK for March 1926, "they had an instinct for what is distinguished; they were rich in the memory of old world places and the knowledge of classics in more than one language; they had the spirit of play, the sentiment that treasures nonsensical possessions, and the humor that keeps alive a family vernacular."

My own first meeting with the Bianco family was in February, 1925, when we showed in The Bookshop for Boys and Girls in Boston an exhibition of Pamela's work and Captain Bianco came over to Boston with Pamela and helped us hang the exhibition. I can see in my mind's eye today Pamela's oils with their special "washed and varnished" look of clearness as they appeared on the walls of the Bookshop's balcony.

Years before, I had read an article about Margery Williams Bianco. The article described her as a tall slender woman who wrote novels, translated from French and Italian into English — and carried snakes in her pocket!

That early article did not make clear, if I remember right, that Margery Bianco had from her earliest years a great interest in natural history and a wonderful understanding of animals.

When I did actually meet Margery, it was at the house Valenti Angelo describes in this book. Her famous pet, "Dear old Peoplecat," as she referred to him in a letter, was living then. It was after his death at seventeen years of age that Margery acquired the Pomeranian, Susan, who greeted Mr. Angelo so cordially.

A letter written in the winter of 1935 when Margery was living in New Preston, Connecticut, speaks of a second cat, 'Monkey,' "as a perfect barometer, for the nights he decides to sleep indoors I know that I must let the faucets drip and fill the stove well. 'People' has no illusions about going out in unpleasant weather. Rain he loves but not cold." A later letter recorded the family's Easter present to her grandson Lorenzo (Pamela's son) of a canary named 'James Jason,' "who (with five rooms in the house) lives naturally and inevitably on my desk, where he is a great comfort even though he scatters seed industriously all over papers and floor, and, unless I bestir myself, it will just as naturally proceed to take root. Then I shall have a beautiful green bower all around me and no need of going to the country!"

In another letter a tortoise was a member of the family, and in still another Margery wrote with her feet in a chair "because Lorenzo's white rat, full of the spring, was too interested in bare toes." These letters show out of what a solid and natural background of everyday living with animals her two books, ALL ABOUT PETS and MORE ABOUT ANIMALS grew. Recently in my own experience they have proved a solace to a small boy who had lost his father and were also read aloud to the enjoyment of a salty, elderly man.

Over a period of several years when she was giving me her advice on such problematical manuscripts for THE HORN BOOK as I chose to send her, Margery's letters were often concerned with these papers. In commenting upon two which had to do with religion for children, she recorded her own point of view:

"God to the child is an extension of the parent . . . God is a child's only natural and satisfying expansion of the universe, a personal God, some one at the head of things. A paper on religion for children today cannot be written at all without touching the particular problem which worries a great many children. If God is beneficent, how come there are wars and massacres and all the disasters of today? This, it seems to me, is the point that must be faced and accounted for somehow. Too many parents at this moment are probably murmuring, 'Well, my dear, . . . and 'When you are a little older,' . . . etc. If you feel that these things are due to man's not keeping faith with God, or to his own greed and misunderstanding, come right out and say so. It is an urgent issue."

Is it not strange that in a world which has seen so many children overwhelmed with the realism of incredible disaster and terror, we should still question the value of imaginative literature for them? In her essay upon the poet, Walter de la Mare, Margery has written in this book such wise words upon this point. She also takes her stand with William Faulkner as to the writer's, and especially the poet's, function.

"There is no privacy deeper or more precious than that in which the spirit finds its inner nourishment . . . I doubt if any child, nurtured on imaginative tales, was ever seriously handicapped in facing the actual world . . . More than ever we have need, today, of the vital quality of imagination and of poetry and of its power to inspire courage and faith, need of 'the music-makers and makers of dreams.' We have need of the poet's vision where our own fails, to be reminded that there are qualities and values less perishable than those which shift and crumble around us."

BERTHA MAHONY MILLER.

January 31, 1951.

CONTENTS

PART ONE

MARGERY BIANCO
HER LIFE AND WORK

1881   MARGERY WILLIAMS BIANCO   1944

MARGERY WILLIAMS BIANCO

By Anne Carroll Moore

I.

SINCE about 1925 the name of Margery Bianco has been associated with a rare quality of criticism and appreciation as well as creative work of unusual character and distinction.

At this time of heightened interest in the interchange of significant books with other countries, I am freshly impressed by the quality and variety of Mrs. Bianco's interests, her skill as a writer and translator, the reliability and richness of her background and, above all, by the wisdom, the humor, the spiritual integrity she brought to the field of children's books after World War I.

In her, as I believe, the *St. Nicholas* of Mary Mapes Dodge might well have found the creative editor so sorely needed at the half-century turn of that lamented magazine. I like to speculate on what a 20th century magazine for children Margery Bianco might have made out of her own love of *St. Nicholas* as a child in London, tempered and expanded by her experience of life in the United States in girlhood, in France, Italy and England after her marriage, and with her children. With an inexhaustible store of first-hand knowledge of literature and of art values, of nature, and of human beings at her command, Mrs. Bianco had also the gift of insight which belongs to the editor who knows the real thing at once. An inexorable critic of her own work and that of others, she knew the cost of creating and inspired confidence in the novice.

I have never known so modest a person who was at the same time so assured, so firmly rooted in sound information, common sense and discriminating taste. As an editor, I never questioned any statement of hers. She *knew* where I might have been guessing. As a writer I received confidence and inspiration from her.

Her influence during the period of rich flowering of children's books in the United States was a very potent one on the authors, artists, editors and librarians and booksellers with whom she came into personal contact.

Editors of children's books in publishing houses were just getting on their sea legs and were eagerly scanning the horizon for just such an author — as Louise Seaman bore eloquent testimony in *The Horn Book* for March 1926. In one of her incomparable bring-the-subject-to-life sketches, Miss Seaman wrote "About the Biancos." She told of her own first awareness of Pamela, whose paintings exhibited at the Leicester Galleries in London in 1919 had been reproduced, accompanied by poems by Walter de la Mare, in *Flora*, published by Heinemann. This beautiful book had been sent to her for review in *The Publishers' Weekly*. Not content with the brief review she was asked to do, Miss Seaman wrote to London to find out more about the child artist. Her letter, answered by Pamela's father, Captain Francesco Bianco, an authority on rare books and fine printing, was soon followed by an invitation to meet the artist herself at the Anderson Galleries in New York, where the paintings were again exhibited in the spring of 1921.

Miss Seaman's intimate sketch of the family was written against the background of Pamela's studio in Macdougal Alley in New York. It was written, too, after the publication of *The Velveteen Rabbit*, *Poor Cecco* and *The Skin Horse*, and after she had secured for Macmillan's Little Library the charming story of *The Little Wooden Doll* for which Pamela had made illustrations years before. The relationship to the family and their pets then established by Miss Seaman bore fruit in *All About Pets*, *More About Animals*, and *Green Grows the Garden*.

In *A Tribute to Margery Bianco* published in the *Elementary English Review* for June, 1935, Louise Seaman Bechtel writes, "These books seem to strike a new note in 'nature writing' for children. An adult would call each chapter a charming essay, but children doubtless read them for the facts about the animals, and plenty of interesting facts and common-sense advice they find." Mrs. Bianco wrote particularly about cats. *All About Pets* is dedicated to "The Common People, who has helped throughout with his encouragement and companionship if not advice." (Common People, a large black cat, was a member of the Bianco family for seventeen years. His portrait is the frontispiece of *More About Animals*.) "Cats are full of secrets and private enterprises of their own," says Mrs. Bianco and she offers convincing proof of how cats talk. "If you had ever seen her with a dog, you'd have another key to her character," says Miss Seaman. "The firmness results in good training and the affection means that the dog will love her forever. It is typical of her that she advises you to talk to your pets. Read the book and see why." Louise Seaman's own love of dogs, her feeling for Rachel Field's beloved Spriggin and Trotty and for her own small dachshund, Mr. Nathaniel Winkle, played no small part in the conception of these books and in stirring memories which led to such delightful true stories as "Spot in the Congo," "Raining Rabbits," and "Spikey and Co." No wonder *More About Animals* is dedicated to her. "She has also interpreted America in a new sort of story," says Miss Seaman in speaking of *The Street of Little Shops* and *The Good Friends*. "We cannot call its humor anything at all but American . . . only some one who has lived in the country and loved it could have written these books."

The fine editorial perception of May Massee was behind these books and others. Miss Massee knew the intrinsic value of so natural an expression of life in books for children and cherished it.

Winterbound, Other People's Houses, Bright Morning and *Forward, Commandos!* had not been published when this tribute by Louise Seaman Bechtel to Margery Bianco was written. Read in the order in which they appeared, they seemed to take their place as parts of a commentary on everyday living which has continuity, serenity, and the practicality born of imaginative understanding and adventurous spirit.

The Velveteen Rabbit has poignant associations for me personally. An unbound copy of the book was sent to me by Eugene Saxton, then chief editorial adviser to the George H. Doran Company, with this query: "Do you think we could sell 1200 copies if we import the sheets?" "If you don't publish it, I will," was my reply. "It belongs in the true Hans Christian Andersen tradition. Who is Margery Williams and how came William Nicholson to illustrate it?"

Mr. Nicholson's character portrait of Queen Victoria with her little dog had been one of my treasures for years and I knew that he had painted some remarkable portraits of children. To associate his name with these fresh interpretive drawings for a children's story gave me a thrill. I was then reviewing children's books for *The Bookman*, published by the Doran Company. Margery Williams, I was told, was the mother of Pamela Bianco. She had published novels under her own name before her marriage, but *The Velveteen Rabbit* was her first children's book. If I wanted to know how Mr. Nicholson happened to make the pictures, I would have to ask him.

I spent the spring and summer of 1921 in a devastated area of northern France and in England, and I paid another short visit to these countries in the fall of 1922. I came back with vivid first-hand impressions of children whose toys and pets and books had been destroyed, and of the apathy of the publishers I met. A notable exception was Mr. Sidney Pawling of Heinemann's, who had fallen in love with the story of *The Velveteen Rabbit*; he believed it to be a classic, and, wishing to give it the very best format he could devise, had persuaded the artist to take it away with him on a holiday. "I felt sure Nicholson couldn't resist it," he said.

The artist confirmed this information when I mustered the courage to go to see him in his studio in Appletree Yard. One had only to spend an hour in that enchanting studio and listen to a flow of refreshing talk to realize that the shabby velveteen rabbit on the chimney piece and the old skin horse who had served as models to some extent, the artist said, had been in his family for years.

Imaginative understanding of the past — the reality of children and their interests in his own life, the timeless magic of transformation — held the secret of his pictures. I came away invigorated and with lively impressions of the Bianco family who had spent a holiday in Wales not far from the Nicholsons. I was to hear more of this delightful holiday from Margery Bianco when we met for the first time in the Children's Room behind the Library Lions. I walked out of Appletree Yard with the precious original drawings under my arm along with two copies of *The Velveteen Rabbit* characteristically inscribed by the artist with an identification tag — one for me and one for the Children's Room where the originals were to be shown as part of the holiday exhibition of 1922. Strolling through St. James Park at dusk in the company of the Nursery Magic Fairy and a joyous family of wild rabbits didn't seem in the least strange to me then.

"You can almost see the Velveteen Rabbit changing into a real one," the children said when they saw the pictures. "Read us the story," begged the two who had lingered after the Christmas Story Hour. And so I read from the very book I had just brought back from London. Out of their listening and the conversation that followed was born the idea of putting Nicholas, the mascot who had accompanied me on my travels, into a book.

Years afterward when we had become very good friends, I told Margery Bianco of that reading in the Fifth Avenue window seat of a room which had grown very dear to her. I told her of the child skeptic who regarded Nicholas as "just a wooden boy" and of the other child who had said, "That's because you don't know enough. He's real to me. I suppose that is the way every story begins — somebody has to believe in it and know enough to write it down. You can do it; just get lots of paper and pencils and keep at it until it is done."

"A wise child! That is all there is to writing a story," said Mrs. Bianco. "It is the believing in it and the keeping at it that are important."

Her respect for children and their opinions was one of her strongest characteristics. She agreed with Kenneth Grahame that children have just as much sense as we have; it is only experience they lack, and she treated her own children and grandchildren accordingly. Clear memory of her own childhood and youth made her relations with all children and young people perfectly natural.

"Lorenzo is a grand companion," she wrote to Bertha Miller of him at the age of seven-and-a-half. "He is back in town with us this winter, after a year in the country, and doing second grade in the public school. He is very gregarious, I am glad to say, and it has been most interesting to see the various friends he has brought home to play with him. We like much the same things and have nice trips every little while to Central Park Zoo or on the El to the Aquarium and Battery Park. India House on the latter route has especially taken his fancy, possibly due to the wonderful smell of coffee which hangs about that region."

"Pamela is doing flower pieces and portraits of Lorenzo which are, I think, the best work she has ever done." From the setting of *Green Grows the Garden* in Connecticut came a delightful letter when Lorenzo was three and a half, telling how much he loved to be read to and of his delight in the drawing of pictures. "It is so enthralling to watch them grow up and they do it so quickly. Already I no longer recognize the baby of half a year past."

In the same year that her finely perceptive paper on de la Mare appeared in *The Horn Book*, she wrote in a personal letter to the editor, "Death should be treated naturally. You don't have to educate children about death. Speak of it as a natural occurrence and they will do the same."

"More than ever, I think, children need imaginative literature as an interpretation. Nature does resist discouragement and not only in the young. The impulse is always toward life and the future. Children are taken up with war and the excitement of it, but it doesn't mean to them what it means to us, unless we make it so. Their own imagination, I think, tends to make of it something like a highly exciting game. It is a defense and like all Nature's defenses, wise. Last night I was reading *My Brother's Face* by Mukerji. Do you know that chapter where, speaking of his mother, he describes the extraordinary gentle wisdom with which she used legend and stories to interpret the spiritual problems of life?"

All her life Margery Bianco so regarded the fairy tales of Hans Christian Andersen. "Everything has a story to tell," she reminded the readers of *The Horn Book* for May, 1927. "Andersen knew this and made no effort to choose the bright side of things, or even to insure a happy ending unless it happens naturally. He wrote of the world about him and of the things in it as colored by his vision."

And this, as I view her work, is exactly what Margery Bianco herself did.

II.

As Margery Williams, she had published her first novel at the age of twenty-one. There is no hint of the amateur in *The Late Returning* (Heinemann 1902). It is an absorbing story of insurrection and conflicting loyalties in a struggle for freedom told with the skill of a young writer who wastes no words. Reading it for the first time in the light of my study of Mrs. Bianco's work, I think it a novel with an appeal to young people of today who have an instinctive feeling for style, characterization and emotional restraint. The book is dedicated to R. W. The initials are those of Robert Williams, the father of Margery, who died when she was seven years old.

Robert Williams was a fellow of Merton College, Oxford, and a distinguished classical scholar of his day. He became a barrister and also a newspaperman — a writer of editorials for *The Daily Telegraph* and *The Observer* and of special articles for *The Times*. He held liberal views concerning the education of children. "My father believed children should be taught to read early and then have no regular teaching until they were ten years old," says Mrs. Bianco. "My favorite book in my father's library was Wood's *Natural History* in three big green volumes, and I knew every reptile, bird and beast in those volumes before I knew the multiplication table."

There can be little doubt that Margery Williams inherited from her father not only the desire to write, but also the instinct for form and sound workmanship which distinguished her work. *Bright Morning*, based on incidents of her childhood happily combined with that of an older sister, reveals the scholarly father in warm human relationship to his family in more than one slight incident. The characters in this little book live for the reader in their city and seaside backgrounds as real people. *Bright Morning* has the freshness of a spring morning in London, and it also holds the joys and terrors of the sea for a child who was always to look upon it with wonder.

The sea is the background of the last of her novels, *The Bar*, published in England in 1906, yet based in a village on the south coast of New Jersey where superstition was rife and a haunted house something more than a stage property. I read this novel and *The Price of Youth* (1904), with its background of New Jersey pine woods and barrens, with interest. True, they are dated as novels, yet each of them has power to stir the imagination, for both are concerned with human problems the author was freshly observing and about which she was thinking. The mystery of Nature, never to lose its wonder for her, is ever present and so is the sensitivity to inanimate things which was to find mature expression in her stories of nursery toys.

When she wrote, "I disliked everything I had written before. I wanted to do something different but did not know what it should be," Margery Bianco had had an experience of life that must have been full of possibilities for a writer of her ability. Fifteen years had passed since the publication of her last novel, and she had published nothing during those years save a small book about Paris (1910).

As one of a series, "Peeps at Great Cities," published in England by A. & C. Black, this little book with its picture plan of Central Paris and its excellent full-page illustrations in color I have just read for the first time, although it has held a place on public library shelves for years. "I read it many times as a child," says Pamela, "for I was too young when we lived in Paris to remember very clearly. I liked the book very much."

It is written from direct observation. A fine selective

instinct governs the choice of material, but there is no writing down to children. "Paris reminds one of a big village," says the author, and proceeds to treat it as a place where she is living and enjoying its small shops and street markets no less than its beautiful gardens and palaces. There must have been a general pattern for the "Peeps," but Margery Bianco held Paris rather than an outline before her. The book has life and color in it and holds suggestion for the writer of children's books about other cities and countries.

"It was by a sort of accident that *The Velveteen Rabbit* became the beginning of all the stories I have written since," says Mrs. Bianco. "By thinking about toys and remembering toys, they suddenly became very much alive — Poor Cecco and all the family toys that had been so much a part of our lives; toys I had loved as a little girl — my almost forgotten Tubby who was the rabbit, and old Dobbin the Skin Horse, the toys my children had loved."

I have always felt that the life tenure of *Poor Cecco*, dedicated to Pamela and Cecco, was threatened by the too elaborate format characteristic of a lavish period. Here, as I think, is a novel in miniature, original and true to form, with a well-defined plot which may some day emerge in a dress better suited to its nature.

In *Winterbound* and in *Other People's Houses*, Mrs. Bianco wrote two books for girls which bid fair to outlive most of the career stories of the time in which they were published. "I wrote these books as experiments," she says, "because I have always been interested in everyday stories as long as they were *real*."

Winterbound is the story of a family faced with a new kind of life in an old house situated in the Connecticut Hills to which they had come to live in order to save money.

It was while making her home in the region of *Winterbound* that Mrs. Bianco also wrote *The Street of Little Shops* (inimitable short stories with interpretive pictures in color), *The Hurdy-Gurdy Man*, so spontaneously illustrated by Robert Lawson, and the lovely *Green Grows the Garden* for which Grace Paull made effective decorations. These books are an expression of American country and village life and character which we may send to other countries with pride.

Of *Other People's Houses*, Mrs. Bianco wrote to Miss Massee:

Other People's Houses is just a plain story of everyday life. It has no trimmings, almost no plot, and it concerns the experience of a girl who wants to earn her living in a city and is willing to try anything that turns up, domestic jobs included, rather than give in.

All over the country there are girls very much like Dale in this book. They are girls who haven't got college degrees or a chance of getting them and have no special training for careers. They aren't likely to blossom out into successful artists or writers overnight, to discover lost wills hidden in old furniture, to inherit odd pieces of property and convert them into thriving business concerns within a year on no capital, to unravel mysteries, save impossible situations through heroism or meet strangers who turn out to be wealthy long-lost uncles. Just what would they do if they wanted to earn a living, and what sort of a time would they have trying it out?

That was the starting point of the story and I have tried to work it out in the way it very probably would happen. I was trying to get away from the average success story which I never felt is playing fair to the reader.

It is significant and characteristic of Margery Bianco's desire to do something new and different in each of her books that the last one, *Forward, Commandos!*, should be concerned with living boys and their natural interests so closely allied to her own. Its crisp dialogue and real understanding of boy nature give it an immediate appeal and assure it an enduring place among boys' books. Her familiarity with New Jersey woods and the fascinations of a tidal river reach back to the novels of her youth of which I have spoken.

The search for reality and the clear sight of one who has lived very close to Nature in all its aspects are to be found in all of Margery Bianco's writings. Economic conditions might threaten as they did during the years of depression, but the integrity of her art was never deflected from its course.

"I write to please myself," she once said when she was asked to give some account of her method to a group of librarians. It is only by writing that one learns to write. Rejection slips had taught her early to take an objective view of her own efforts.

I have dwelt at length upon Mrs. Bianco's work at this time because I feel it important that her books be kept in print and made more widely known to writers and students of literature for children as well as to children of the postwar world.

"Imagination is only another word for the interpretation of life," Margery Bianco reminds us in her own tribute to de la Mare. "It is through imagination that a child makes his most significant contacts with the world about him, that he learns tolerance, pity, understanding and the love for all created things."

I give back these words in her memory.

BOOKS BY
MARGERY WILLIAMS BIANCO

Arranged chronologically

The Late Returning. London. 1902. Heinemann. o.p.

The Price of Youth. London and New York. 1904. Macmillan. o.p.

The Bar. London. 1906. Methuen. o.p.

Paris. (Peeps at Great Cities Series.) London. 1910. Adam and Charles Black.

The Velveteen Rabbit. Illustrated by William Nicholson. London. 1922. Heinemann. New York. 1926. Doubleday.

Poor Cecco. Illustrated by Arthur Rackham. New York. 1925. Doubleday. o.p.

The Little Wooden Doll. Illustrated by Pamela Bianco. New York. 1925. Macmillan.

The Apple Tree. With decorations by Boris Artzybasheff. New York. 1926. George H. Doran Company. o.p.

The Skin Horse. Illustrated by Pamela Bianco. New York. 1927. Doubleday. o.p.

The Adventures of Andy. Illustrated by Leon Underwood. New York. 1927. George H. Doran Company. o.p.

All About Pets. New York. 1929. Macmillan.

The Candlestick. Illustrated by Ludovic Rodo. New York. 1929. Doubleday. o.p.

The House That Grew Smaller. Illustrated by Rachel Field. New York. 1931. Macmillan. o.p.

The Street of Little Shops. Illustrated by Grace Paull. New York. 1932. Doubleday.

The Hurdy-Gurdy Man. Illustrated by Robert Lawson. New York. 1933. Oxford. o.p.

The Good Friends. Illustrated by Grace Paull. New York. 1934. Viking. o.p.

More about Animals. Illustrated by Helen Torrey. New York. 1934. Macmillan.

Green Grows the Garden. Illustrated by Grace Paull. New York. 1936. Macmillan. o.p.

Winterbound. Decorations by Kate Seredy. New York. 1936. Viking.

Other People's Houses. New York. 1939. Viking.

Franzi and Gizi. Illustrated by Gisella Loeffler. New York. 1941. Messner. o.p.

Bright Morning. Drawings by Margaret Platt. New York. 1942. Viking.

Forward, Commandos! Illustrated by Rafaello Busoni. New York. 1944. Viking.

BOOKS TRANSLATED BY MARGERY BIANCO

Juniper Farm. Translated from the French of René Bazin. New York. 1928. Macmillan.

Little Black Stories. Translated from the French of Blaise Cendrars. Illustrated from woodblocks by Pierre Pinsard. New York. 1929. Payson & Clarke. o.p.

The African Saga. Translated from the French of Blaise Cendrars. New York. 1927. Payson & Clarke. o.p.

Rufus, the Fox. Adapted from the French of Samivel. New York. 1937. Harper. o.p.

HER CHILDREN LONG AGO

By Pamela Bianco

LTHOUGH my brother Cecco and I were both born in London, the earliest home I can remember is our last Paris apartment at 16 Rue Mayet, with its long dim corridor. Cecco, a year and a half older than myself, can remember a still earlier Paris apartment, into which my parents moved when I was an infant, and which my mother usually referred to later as the Toy Cupboard Flat.

On top of my mother's tall drop-leaf desk in the Rue Mayet apartment was a beautiful old French clock with two bronze cupids, one on either side of the dial. Cecco and I made up a game about them: we pretended that the one wearing a wreath of grapes around his head belonged to Cecco, and that the one wearing a wreath of roses was mine. We were both so small then we had to stand upon chairs in order to talk to them properly. On top of another tall desk, this one of ebony, lived my mother's pet white rat Narcissus, whom I called Mousissus.

Every afternoon Cecco and I played in the Luxembourg Gardens; and occasionally upon a Sunday my father, a bibliographer, then manager of the rare book department of Brentano's in Paris, would take us all for a picnic in the woods of Fontainebleau.

In the nursery were a sack of wooden blocks, an immense rocking-horse with rosettes, Cecco's wooden dog, Poor Cecco, and my teddy bear, Petercat. Poor Cecco must have been given to my brother at a very early age, for I cannot remember a time when he did not exist.

When let down the drop-leaf of my mother's desk was green baize inside. Sometimes she wrote properly at her desk, but most of the time she would sit holding the manuscript upon her lap, in different rooms of the apartment. I think it was because she was so often interrupted in those days, and obliged to drop her writing at a moment's notice. Often it was because Cecco or I asked her to make a drawing for us. I usually asked my mother to draw me a Christmas tree; this she would do time after time, with all the presents hanging upon it. Sometimes Cecco and I might ask for paper toys instead, and then my mother would tear a sheet of paper out of her manuscript book, and after she had folded it a number of different ways it would become a boat with two seats, or a tea kettle one might boil water in over a candle.

In those days my mother made her own manuscript books from large sheets of very shiny pale yellow paper, which she folded and sewed together. All her life she had a preference for writing upon yellow paper.

In Paris my mother read some beautiful fairy stories to us from a book by Mary de Morgan, entitled *On a Pincushion*.

Our four years in Paris were interrupted for Cecco and myself by a visit to the United States. My mother took us over and left us in the care of her elder sister Cecil, married to an American artist, Edward Boulton. Cecco and I lived in New Jersey for about a year; it was Aunt Cecil who brought us back to Paris again.

I must have been four and a half years old when we went to live in Golder's Green in London, for I remember having my fifth birthday in Lucas Square. It falls during Christmas week, and that afternoon as a cambric tea time surprise, my mother decorated a tiny tree with crimson crepe paper.

There was very little automobile traffic in Golder's Green in those days, since most of the tradesmen's wagons were drawn by horses. Cecco and I were allowed to wander wherever we liked, as long as we told my mother where we were going. Our favorite playground was a great open space which we called the Valley, where new houses were being built.

Sunday morning walks were usually upon Hampstead Heath with my parents. Cecco and my father and I always started on ahead, and a little later, after she had put Sunday dinner in the oven, my mother would join us there. One Sunday morning she arrived upon the Heath carrying a little dead mole which she had found by the wayside. Neither Cecco nor I had ever seen one before. My mother explained to us that moles are blind, and that afternoon Cecco and I gave him a funeral in the garden. Upon his tombstone we wrote:

> In this dark hole
> Lies Mr. Mole.
> He died of fright
> Because he had no sight.

The little mole's funeral was followed by a party with refreshments.

After Dorothy, our governess, came to live with us, Cecco and I took long walks with her every afternoon, upon asphalted roads whose sidewalks were bordered with May bushes and laburnum trees. In the mornings Dorothy gave us lessons.

In those days our hero was Captain Scott, the Antarctic explorer. Cecco and I made up a long poem about him which ended:

> To Captain Scott the angels came soon
> And carried him up by the light of the moon.

During the time we lived in Golder's Green my father had a shop in Charing Cross, where he sold old and rare books. One day he discovered a very rare book printed by William Caxton, and in order to celebrate its sale he bought my mother a brindled English bulldog, whom she named Caxton.

My mother always encouraged us to keep pets. Starting from the Golder's Green days, Cecco and I owned a series of hedgehogs, guinea pigs and rabbits. Usually they came in pairs, Cecco's being named Paul, and mine Virginia. In addition to our pets Cecco and I had little garden plots, and in winter a hyacinth bulb each to watch growing in water.

When I was five years old my father taught me the poetry of William Butler Yeats. I used to recite, "When I play on my fiddle in Dooney," to him.

One night in Golder's Green, long after I had fallen asleep, Dorothy woke me up again and handed me a beautiful doll with pale golden hair. It was a present from Uncle Angelo, who had just arrived on a visit from Italy. I was carried downstairs into the sitting room to greet him.

Uncle Angelo was my father's younger brother. He had a delightful sense of humor, and during this visit to Golder's Green, used to join Cecco and myself in many of our games. Later, when we went to live in Italy, Uncle Angelo was to be our constant friend and companion. He survived the First World War, serving in the front line trenches, only to die under tragic circumstances not long after we left Italy.

I named the doll Uncle Angelo gave me Daisy, but somehow I never played with her as I did with Tubby, of whom my mother wrote in *Poor Cecco*. Tubby, half teddy bear, half cat, and her sister Fluffy were my cherished playthings. For them I spent endless hours sewing elaborate dresses. Bulka, who had two reincarnations, belonged to Cecco, and was named after Count Tolstoi's dog. The first two Bulkas were china bulldog banks that broke, but Bulka the third was made of more durable papier-mâché. Later, when he wore out in Turin, my mother re-covered him in gold-colored cloth, and Tubby and Fluffy were re-covered at the same time to match. My mother always treated our toys as though they were just as real to her as they were to us. Once when I was away on a visit she wrote:

"The Tubbies are very well and happy. As a matter of fact, they are in Tubbyland now, as Jensina's mother telephoned to ask if they couldn't stay over Wednesday, so as to go to a picnic which she had arranged — with dancing afterwards, and I felt sure you wouldn't mind."

After we had been living in Golder's Green for nearly three years, my father and mother took a trip to Italy, leaving Cecco and myself in the care of my English grandmother. One day a letter arrived from my mother, telling us that my father had been appointed director of a film company in Turin, and that we were going to live in Italy. In her letter my mother described the villa in which we would spend that first summer. It was upon a high hill, she wrote, and the garden was full of rose bushes.

When the time came to leave Golder's Green Cecco

and I packed Tubby, Fluffy, Poor Cecco, and Bulka in the trunk, and Caxton climbed in on top of them and lay there, afraid we might leave without him.

Villa Gilli was in the hills just outside Turin, and when we arrived it was just as my mother had described: it seemed as though every rose in the world grew inside that immense garden, and they were all in blossom. I woke up very early the first morning and went downstairs. Uncle Angelo was making coffee over a spirit lamp, the only other person awake. He said, "You are in Italy now, so you will have to talk in Italian to me." And then he told me what everything in the dining room was called.

Uncle Angelo worked with my father at the Corona Film Company. He and my father left Villa Gilli early every morning to go to the office, and in the evening Cecco and I would walk down a long shadowy avenue to the villa gates to meet them upon their return.

Besides Uncle Angelo, our Italian grandmother, whom we called Nonna, and Aunt Letizia, my father's sister, stayed in the villa with us, through a part of that summer. Aunt Letizia, gentle and deeply religious, was employed in the Turin offices of the Italian State Railway. She always took great delight in telling Cecco and myself fairy tales.

That autumn we moved into an apartment in Turin at 21 Via Cassini. It was to be our home for the next six years. Cecco had a bedroom wallpapered in green, my bedroom had pink wallpaper. Between our bedrooms was a room we called the light room, because it had a tall glass door leading onto a balcony overlooking the garden, and was usually filled with sunlight. My mother kept her sewing machine in the light room, and on winter mornings would sit there in the sunlight with her embroidery frame, for she made exquisite filet lace and Venetian point in those days.

One day a magnificent doll's house was delivered to 21 Via Cassini and brought into the light room. It had been constructed upon my father's orders by one of the stage designers of the Corona Film Company, and resembled an immense apartment house. My father, then on a London visit, wrote : "I hope they have brought you the doll's house by this time. Personally I think it is much too wonderful a thing for a simple doll like yours."

Not long after we had moved into Via Cassini Cecco and I were enrolled in a little private school called the Istituto Bracco, where the pupils all wore white pinafores. Our maid Rosina used to accompany us there and back twice a day; we walked along Corso Vinzaglio, an avenue with horse chestnut trees on either side.

Once a week, instead of Rosina, Aunt Letizia would fetch us at noon and take us back to Nonna's apartment for lunch. The apartment in which Nonna lived with Aunt Letizia and Uncle Angelo was on the top floor of a very old Turin house. To reach it one had to climb up a wide stone staircase that always smelled of flowers, because the tenants on the first floor kept a perfume factory.

I was never very happy at school, and after the first year my mother let me stay at home and gave me lessons herself. She taught me French, and English literature, besides a variety of other subjects. I also used to read aloud to her from the Bible.

Before very long Cecco outgrew the Istituto Bracco, and passed on to the Ginnasio.

In Turin my mother gave me the little writing desk which had belonged to her when she was a child. It was an antique, exquisitely inlaid box, with two compartments inside, whose lids formed a red velvet slope upon which to write. My mother had written stories upon it in her childhood. I was very proud of that little desk; in one of the compartments I kept a long novel about white mice, which I spent several years writing, in the other a sheaf of poems.

We never returned to Villa Gilli. Our second Italian summer was spent at Valprato, up in the Alps, and the summer following we stayed at Cumiana on the family estate of the Casanovas, our close friends and apartment neighbors in Via Cassini. In Cumiana my father originated the idea of a weekly competition. During the week Cecco and I would prepare little story books, or sometimes a drawing, and when he came up on weekends my father would award a prize for the best.

Because of the war we did not leave Turin again, except for short visits, after that third summer. Instead long afternoons were spent in the Valentino Gardens, and upon the banks of the River Po. And every year in the early spring my mother and Cecco and I would make an expedition up a hill just outside Turin, named San Vito, to pick the first violets and primroses. Caxton always accompanied us on these trips. During the last year of the war Cecco and I made tiny bunches of violets, writing a letter to hide inside each, and sent them to the soldiers at the British Military Hospital.

I do not believe I became fully aware of the war and all that it meant, until the last two years of it. Things then became very difficult. There was little food to be had, and we were never warm enough. My mother made two calico bags, inside which Cecco and I kept our daily rations of bread.

Uncle Angelo was away at the front, his unexpected leaves being always a source of great joy to us. On one occasion, while home on leave, Uncle Angelo wrote out a contract under whose terms Cecco and I were each to make one drawing a week for him, and send it to him in the trenches. It was the first contract Cecco and I had ever signed, and Uncle Angelo took great delight in adorning it with long legal words.

It was not long before my father was also called up for military duty. He became a captain in the Italian army and was stationed through one winter as commander in a military prison, high up in the cold mountains at Fenestrelle. Later he was appointed supervisor in the rice-growing district of Vercelli.

Life in Turin became increasingly difficult. Through the long winter months we lived in one room of the apartment. My mother gave English lessons in order to make ends meet. And once a week she helped the matron in the linen room of the British Military Hospital.

Towards the end of the war Nonna suffered a stroke, from which she only partially recovered, remaining an invalid until her death a few years later.

At about the time the war ended I gave up playing with my toys, and began to draw every day instead. My father was still in uniform, but living at home now. In the early summer mornings, before it was time for him to report for duty, he and Cecco and I would go bicycle riding in the beautiful country surrounding Turin.

In the late winter following the Armistice, my father took a trip to London, and not long after he had left I was invited by an artist friend of his, named Petrella da Bologna, to visit him in San Remo.

While I was in San Remo I received many letters from my mother. They were filled with news of Cecco and herself, of Caxton, and of the guinea pig and four pet mice I had left in her care. Of our bulldog she wrote:

"Poor Caxton has rheumatism badly, can hardly walk, and has to be lifted in and out of chairs. Cecco and I went for a walk up San Vito on Tuesday (without Caxton, for we had to bring him home when we reached the Mauriziano) and found quite a lot of primroses and some blue flowers and snowdrops. It was very hot up there, and we ate tea in the field at the top. There a bee kept buzzing round, so first we gave it chocolate and it ate some, and then Cecco made a paper cup of water for it and it drank a lot, and kept coming back every little while to drink again."

Later my mother wrote:

"Caxton is still quite bad, I'm sorry to say — he can hardly use his hind legs at all, they bend under him when he tries to walk — he lies on his cushion on the bed nearly all day."

In another letter my mother told me of an afternoon spent in the Turin museums:

"Yesterday Angelo and Cecco and I started out to go to the Egyptian Museum. We waited ever so long for a tram and then found out there weren't any on account of the strike, so we had to walk. It was fearfully hot, but we got there finally, spent a long time looking at the Egyptian sculptures (there are some lovely small statues) and then went up to the Pinacoteca to see the pictures, and we saw the Botticellis. They are beautiful. And there was one in the next room, I think, a Madonna and Child which I liked so much. You are sure to remember it, but I can't remember the name just now to tell you, small and square, hung rather high. There are some lovely things there and I would have liked to stay longer, but it was 4 o'clock then so we had to go, and as we were still very hot and tired Angelo took us to Pepino's to get an ice before we started to walk back."

From my father in London I also received a number of letters. Many of them were concerned with my work, for I was drawing steadily then, and sending the drawings over to him. It was during this time that my first exhibition of drawings at the Leicester Galleries took place.

One day my father wrote:

"I have sent Mammy a beautiful book of poetry entitled *Peacock Pie*, by a great English poet called Walter de la Mare. His verses are very very beautiful."

Not long afterwards my mother forwarded *Peacock Pie* to me in San Remo, and I then had the delight of reading Walter de la Mare's poetry for the first time.

In the early summer Cecco came to San Remo to be with me. He was badly in need of sea air and sunshine, for he had never fully regained his strength after a fever which had kept him in bed for many weeks during the previous autumn.

And now in her letters my mother spoke of our going to live in London before very long. She was already then sorting and putting things in order for a not too far away departure; and sometime during those same days our faithful Caxton, an elderly and ill dog, must have been put to sleep, because, when my mother joined us in San Remo in July, he was not with her.

My father did not return from England until late summer. He came directly to San Remo, and in the autumn we all went back to Turin.

Uncle Angelo, no longer in uniform, was employed with a steel company. Cecco and I visited him in his new office, and, as during earlier days, he took us for walks in his free time.

But our stay in Turin was brief. Soon everything was in readiness for us to go and live in England. This time I did not pack the Tubbies, for I had given up playing with them; they remained in Italy with Aunt Letizia.

Uncle Angelo came to Porta Nuova, the Turin station, to see us off. He was carrying a frail filled with red apples for us to eat on the train, and we said good-bye to him then for the last time.

Childhood ended with our leaving Italy. And since that faraway afternoon I have returned to Via Cassini only in my dreams.

A LIVING FRIENDSHIP

By Valenti Angelo

 N the East Side in New York City there is a
house. There is nothing very unusual about
this particular house. It is like hundreds of
other houses on the East Side, houses that
have survived an era never again to be seen
nor experienced in our modern times, an era of family dwellings, of friendship, of close ties between neighbors, before
the invasion of the super-family units, which today have
mechanized and indexed thousands of families into snug,
efficient quarters, resembling the dwellings of a new species
which one might label as the human ant.

The house of which I want to speak is of special interest
to me because it was there I became acquainted with
Margery Williams Bianco.

It was in 1937 that I made her acquaintance. I feel that
I must describe this house because of the many pleasant
hours spent there, and also of the many impressions which,
although they are now but memories, have deeply enriched

my belief that friendship is above all the most treasured thing in all the world.

The house is three stories high with a cream-colored, weather-beaten stucco front. The once bright blue trim around high arched windows which face south and the street are now faded. Faded too are the variegated wooden shutters, but from behind each shutter the brilliance of floriated sky blue curtains breathe new life into the street. A few potted plants lend the dwelling a touch of gaiety. The entrance way to the dwelling, with its recessed vestibule, is somewhat imposing: heavy, double, oaken door, a fan-shaped transit window of amber glass reflects the tenements across the street. A ball from the hand of some future baseball star which had missed its intended mark left a jagged hole in the transit. No one bothered to repair the pane of glass. The appearance of the hole impairs in no way the quiet atmosphere within. And in no way does it seem to deface the dignity of the humble dwelling.

As I studied the house from across the street one spring day in 1937, I began to ponder on the lives of authors. I did so because from that day on, without my knowledge of it, I too was to become an author.

Carrying the many-times-revised, page-frayed manuscript of my first book, *Nino*, I started across the street. A group of children playing on the doorsteps gave me no notice. They went on with their games. Stepping gingerly among them I reached the door. I stood there a moment as memories of some years passed through my mind. These memories were concerned with Margery Bianco, who through those years had not been totally unknown to me. I became acquainted with her writing through *The Skin Horse*, a small book published in 1927.

It was really through the drawings made for this little book by her gifted daughter, Pamela Bianco, that I first learned of Margery's writing. I fell deeply in love with both the drawings and the story, and as time passed, learned more about this author's work. For in Margery's writing as well as the drawings of Pamela, I discovered a rarity seldom found in literature and pictures made for children in those days. There was something about her work which seemed to fit my nature. It stuck there, and I nourished the thought that some day I might have the good fortune to meet these two people who had aroused in me a desire to look into more books made for children.

It will sound fantastic perhaps to say that one can readily make friends with the work of another, or even to fall completely in love with it. It is nevertheless true, for in my case it was not only a matter of friendship, but a case of love at first sight. And as I touched my finger to the doorbell, I had a sincere feeling that I was about to meet an old acquaintance — a friend whom I had loved through the years in my imagination. One whom I knew I would love from that day on.

The sound of the doorbell brought the sound of a dog

barking from somewhere in the interior of the house. High-pitched and excited was the dog's voice, and I knew it to be no furious animal. In fact, the bark seemed filled with anticipation mixed with a happiness, as though to warn the visitor well in advance that the dwelling was a friendly one. I felt glad, for I have learned to know the bark of dogs.

If there is magic at all in the sight of one's eyes, Margery Bianco possessed just such a magic. Eyes, soft brown and mellow, filled with a depth of kindness and understanding that seemed to speak long before the tongue. I had never before encountered such unusual eyes. Eyes which emanated a quiet passion, wisdom, and affection.

There was a graciousness about her I am unable to express here because it is now so deeply rooted in me. Words alone are not sufficient to give vent to my feelings. But this I must say in humble sincerity — whatever it was Margery Bianco possessed and gave abundantly to others is needed desperately among people today.

I had come to Margery Bianco for advice and guidance in the matter of writing. She had already read my story which the publishers had sent to her for editorial work. Now I awaited the verdict. I had never written a book and felt my efforts to be feeble. I knew that a judgment must be passed on the work by someone with more knowledge and experience in grammar, composition, punctuation, and so on than I had. My two years of schooling had not been sufficient to give me the confidence needed in the matter of English.

I knew I had a story to tell, but I had no faith in my manner of telling. So good fortune led me to the home of Margery Bianco. It is strange how much one leans on others, when actually, as sooner or later one realizes, the strongest support comes not from the outside but from within oneself.

Margery Bianco pointedly told me as much during that afternoon visit, and for that lesson I was deeply grateful. It was a visit which I can relive vividly, because on that day I learned that in order to be a writer one must have a great deal of patience and understanding, particularly with oneself. Margery made everything seem clear and simple in the most natural way I have ever known. "Be yourself," she would say.

"But" — I was full of buts that afternoon and repeatedly told her my story was full of errors, enough to put the Book of Sin to shame. That I had not succeeded in telling my story as it should have been told. "Don't be silly," she said. "It's your story. I've read it. I like it." Again her eyes expressed that rare sincerity. "All of us make errors," she said. "You should read my books." I smiled, feeling ashamed. "Errors," she continued quietly, "are necessary evils. Without them there could be no corrections. Imagine how dull perfection must be. Errors serve as good experience. Errors can be corrected. And in their correction produce a greater understanding of things. Just be yourself."

As she spoke she convinced me that the faults in my book were largely grammatical. That the important thing was the play, the story. The sincerity. "You have had something to say — to impart to others. You have said your say in the only way you know. What more?"

Again I say, that that first visit enriched my life. There was something noble about it all. And I am grateful to have been a part of it.

Memories are perhaps the most valuable, the dearest and the most cherished things in one's life. If the memories are of such nature that the source of them has added joy, happiness, and enrichment to your life, it will be difficult for you to forget them. For memories have a strange power, a natural power, to reproduce sights, sounds, experiences, and as time wears on, make them grow more vivid, stronger and more profound. And since time itself is a sort of scale or measure by which we are able to weigh the past and thereby judge the present, and at times catch a glimpse into the future, memories play an important part in the time of one's life. Of the many memories by which we, at one time or another, relive the past, there is no doubt that those sprung from friendship are the most treasured.

The afternoon sun streamed into the room from the high arched windows, golden and peaceful. The many shouts coming from children at play in the street fitted into the picture. As we spoke about children, parents, and stories written for children, a warmth of feeling enveloped the room. I knew and felt in the presence of Margery Bianco that here was a person — an ageless person — who not only loved youth, with all its minor idiosyncrasies but also had a great faculty for understanding it.

Everything seemed right on that afternoon. Even Susan, the little Pomeranian, who had so ardently and affectionately barked her greetings on my entry, seemed to say, "Be yourself." Nestled close to Margery, Susan listened to our conversation. In all probability she was thinking how silly it was of me to be so concerned over the simple matter of storytelling.

As the afternoon wore on I learned that Margery Bianco's philosophy was a simple one, easy to understand, earthy and wholesome, imbued with a sensitive view of life and the world as a whole. Her personality at no time seemed to deviate from the simplicity and honesty of thought which was, during those trying years of depression and struggle, being imperiled by the many "isms" and supposedly new styles in every mode of life, and especially in that of the art of writing. Later on when I read *Other People's Houses*, *Winterbound*, and others of her books, I found in them that same philosophy. One of understanding of the meaning of life, and of what constitutes the highest good. To find this trend of thought in books for children is something for which we all should be grateful. In their deep-felt excursions into a life now threatened by up-heaval and unrest, these stories have a power to make the young reader live and glory in the living.

Many writers, I learned later, follow the leader or who-ever happens to be dominant at the moment, thereby neg-lecting a duty to their art and to themselves. This was never true of Margery Bianco.

The knowledge and understanding of the nature of things she expressed in her work enriched the lives of others. Her insight into the animal world was uncanny, as proved by the books *All About Pets*, *More About Animals*, and *The Good Friends*. She possessed a sense of humor devoid of the burdensome drollery which so many clever authors have exercised in order to gain attention. What conclu-sions she arrived at concerning the likes and dislikes of children are summed up in the paper written by her for *The Bookman*, November 1925, and included in this book.

When I left Margery Bianco's house that day, I knew that I had learned many things. I also felt that I had re-newed an old acquaintance. To me it seemed, even long after that visit, that in this world there is no such thing as meeting and parting in friendship. The visits that followed were many. The years that followed made richer the friend-ship between us. The thread of friendship — of delicate fiber and easily severed — seemed to grow stronger. I feel honored to have been among her many friends.

Margery Bianco will always be alive to me, and to all

her friends. No person who has left to the world of literature for children such wisdom and sympathy and love of Nature will ever die. Her work should not go unnoticed in time to come. There is a great need for her kind of writing today, for her work is reaching for some lost dignity in life, and in reaching helps to bring it back.

PART TWO

SELECTIONS FROM THE WRITING
OF MARGERY BIANCO

OUR YOUNGEST CRITICS

By Margery Bianco

IF an actor were called upon to produce a
play, entirely alone, and before an audience
at once eager to be amused yet highly skepti-
cal of the deliberate attempt to amuse; un-
certain of what it does want but amazingly
definite as to what it does not; demanding continual diver-
sion and surprise; appreciative of results when they come
out right but wholly devoid of that weakness which makes
us bear with an artist through sympathy either with himself or with what he is trying to do; and not bound by any
canons of mere politeness to remain if the play does not
please — that actor, I imagine, would be very much in the
position of the author who deliberately sets out to write
a story that will please children.

I say "deliberately," because there it seems to me you
have the root of the whole question. Nothing is easier
than to write a story for children; few things harder, as any
writer knows, than to achieve a story that children will

really like. Between the two lies that great mass of literature, often charmingly written, instructive, attractive, con-
taining apparently every element that should appeal to
the child mind yet destined, for no reason that its creators
can see, to remain nicely kept upon the nursery or library
shelves, while the public for whom it is intended thanks
us politely and returns to the comic strips.

It isn't that children are not easily pleased. They are the
most eager and receptive audience that anyone can have.
They are pleased, as any adult knows, by the most absurd
and ridiculous things; and being pleased by these things
once, they will continue to enjoy them to the end of time
— but they are not always pleased by the very thing that we
think is going to please them. For this reason, one is inclined to believe that the really successful children's book
is just a thing that happens; that it is very rarely the result
of deliberate plan or foresight or, if it began that way, that
it took, somewhere, a mysterious turn of its own in the
making. Just as we might imagine our actor, if he were
a good actor and his play any sort of real play, becoming
so engrossed in it that at a certain point he would forget
all efforts to please his audience, would consign it to
oblivion, and simply go ahead and do the thing to please
himself, only to find perhaps at the end that his audience
was for the first time really with him.

Children are extraordinarily quick to detect any effort
to engage their attention. They have at times an almost dia-

bolical clairvoyance and skepticism regarding the grown-up's intention; they are eternally suspicious and ready to jump the other way. Say to any intelligent person of four or five years, "Look at the pretty flower!" and he will, unless he is a hypocrite or hampered by mere politeness, give you a blank pitying stare or else turn his back. Not that he doesn't appreciate the flower; it is simply that, approached directly, his instinct is to question your motive and suspect some design on his personal liberty. To engage children's interest in anything you have to be keenly interested in that thing yourself; if you are not, if you are merely pretending or playing up to them, they will promptly catch you out.

There are two things the storyteller can always count on with some degree of certainty, love of adventure and love of surprise — the kind of surprise that is really an open secret between the inventor and the listener, something which the listener has all the joy of expecting beforehand and can await trustfully, knowing that after whatever suspense of complication it will unfailingly appear, at just the right moment and with all the accumulated dramatic effect. Children love to be taken, as it were, into the writer's confidence. However often the miracle appears, it will never miss fire. The author of *Swiss Family Robinson* realized this to perfection. He knew that the child mind would follow him faithfully through pages of tedious moralizing, through veritable morasses of instruction, solely for the joy of seeing the needle-and-thread tree perform its useful little stunt just at the very moment when it becomes imperative for the boys to have new trousers, or Mother Robinson's famous reticule — which must have exceeded a pantechnicon in capacity — yield up, in the instant of emergency or discouragement, just the one article without which family life could not proceed. I would wager that whatever the grown-up reader may have forgotten of *Swiss Family Robinson*, he will not have forgotten that reticule.

But the surprise must always be a logical one; it must arise out of something indicated beforehand, not merely happen like that, for no reason, out of a clear sky. I think a good many writers for children are apt to forget this, to think that invention may consist of a series of quite unrelated and extravagant incidents, that imagination simply means having anything at all happen at any moment you like; whereas if true invention lies anywhere it lies in making the utmost use of very definitely limited means, and imagination which does not spring from some correlation of ideas is apt to be just about as interesting as delirium. In a world where anything at all can happen, nothing can ever be surprising. In other words, there's no sort of fun about it.

The child mind is far more logical and orderly, far more concerned with the value of realities, than is sometimes supposed. It is concerned with them, in fact, very intensely and stubbornly, and it is ready to preserve and defend them at all cost. The fact that these realities may differ from our own has no bearing on the question. To the child a doll, let us say, may have an existence quite apart from its material one. The laws of that existence are to her quite clear and definite. To the grownup, whose attitude toward the whole thing is that of concession to the child's imagination, these laws do not exist. He cannot see why, if a doll is assumed to do certain things, it cannot do certain others. He will never, for instance, realize the enormity of making a doll stand on its head or fly through the air.

In the world of imagination these same laws hold good; you cannot successfully evade them. Here everything must be on scale, everything preserve its own definite characteristics. You must observe the conventions. It is a game in which the author is expected to play fair. Your ship must not at a certain moment become an airplane; your crocodile's egg cannot, without serious danger, suddenly bring forth an elephant or a fairy princess, though it may hatch as sophisticated and unsaurian a crocodile as you like. If your stage setting is a forest all that happens in it, however fantastic or nonsensical, must be evolved strictly from the materials and possibilities of that forest and from nowhere else. Thus and in no other way did Cinderella's fairy godmother produce the fairy coach from the resources of the kitchen, and its real appeal to the child mind lies in its being a pumpkin, not in its being a coach, and in the fact that it was drawn by rats and not by horses.

Children will usually respond immediately to any association of the fantastic with the commonplace. The goblin in the enchanted forest isn't nearly so thrilling as the goblin in the tea kettle, or the little man who lives behind the kitchen cupboard and squeaks whenever the door is opened.

What appeals to children is not so much adventure in its wider sense as the possibility of adventure in everyday surroundings and among everyday things — something that might, by a happy chance, conceivably happen in their own lives. It is not the cavern on a remote mountain top but the rabbit hole and the parlor looking glass that are the true gates of romance. And not for nothing has the harlequinade, one of the oldest of all magic plays, been staged invariably outside a prosaic grocer shop in a most prosaic street.

If one goes back to the old classical fairy tales, the ones that most children like the best will be found to be "Little Red Riding Hood," "Cinderella," and "Jack and the Beanstalk." Here, in each case, we have the mysterious and dramatic arising unexpectedly out of quite commonplace circumstances. Any little girl may go on an errand to her grandmother, any little boy plant a row of beans in his mother's back garden, any small household drudge sit at home and dream of the party to which she hasn't been invited.

Details loom very important in a child's mind, especially

with young children. If there was a supper they want to know exactly what everyone had to eat and how much of it; they insist on knowing whether the baby elephant was so big, or only so big. They have in fact a passion for detail and verisimilitude which is not so very far removed in kind from the passion of the confirmed detective story reader — which by the way has nothing to do with mere hunger for the sensational. Not only is the shape, color, or size of things of such importance to them that they will hold up an exciting narrative in order to have some minor point of this nature determined, definitely and beyond doubt, but they do seem to get a real thrill from facts as facts, apart from any relative value to the story. How else account for the absorption with which they will devour page after page of minutiae which to older minds would appear about as exciting as a trade catalogue. However much detail you put in a story, you can seldom put enough to satisfy a child. I am convinced that the popularity even today, among such children as are lucky enough to possess them, of the "Harry and Lucy Book" (known in the family under that title but I believe collectively called *Early Lessons* by Maria Edgeworth), of *Mr. Rutherford's Children* and other books of much the same period, is due very largely to the hypnotic effect induced by their minute chronicling of the events of one single day in a child's life, from putting on his shoes and socks to going to bed, and the manner in which each incident is given its due and proper importance. Far from prosy, they are filled with a wealth of detail the value of which later writers are sometimes inclined to overlook. They produce an effect of reality which brings them very near to the child's own life. Whatever tinge of priggishness these early little heroes and heroines may possess to later minds, they were at least very human, very solid, very actual. They did real things in a real way, they yielded to foolishness and curiosity and conceit as well as to more generous impulses, their experiments came out wrong and their foolishness was laughed at, and it is this, and not their moralizing and fine sentiments, that makes them so alive today. As to moralizing, I don't believe children mind it half so much as is frequently supposed.

They have certainly a very clear sense of justice. Things must in the end come out right. They take a healthy pleasure in seeing the wicked punished, or at least frustrated, and they have an equally healthy dislike of unnecessary tragedy, or of having their feelings harrowed merely for the exigencies of the story. It is taking an unfair advantage. They prefer in the main stories about happy people and happy things, and thus they go back in their demand to the original purpose of a story, which after all is to entertain. And I think on the whole they thoroughly despise sentimentality.

It is true that some of the most beautiful stories ever written for children, including the greater number of Hans Andersen's, have been sad stories. But it is the sadness which is inseparable from life, which has to do with growth and change and impermanence, and with the very essence of beauty. These after all are conceptions of the older mind. It is quite possible that to the child, so far as he is aware of them, those things may not be sad at all: they may be quite natural and inevitable, and just as they should be — perhaps his way of looking at them, and not ours, is the right one. Possibly what his mind grasps is really the essential truth. The Little Fir Tree did have a happy time while it lasted, and after all its memories and regrets of lost youth it did ultimately finish in a blaze of light, and that final glory may just as well have been the flame of life as the pyre of death.

There is a very real satisfaction in writing for children. They are both deeply appreciative and highly critical. Before them the author is put on his mettle. They refuse to be sidetracked by any mere exercise of art. All those skilful embroiderings and unessentials, the nice picking of phrases and building up of "atmosphere" which he may fall back upon to cover an awkward gap or to get away with a story which he knows to be fundamentally weak, are perfectly useless; through them all his emptiness will be revealed. To these critics style means very little. They care more for the thing itself than for how it is done, and they are the one audience whom you cannot hoodwink nor deceive. Unless your story is there no ingenious juggling with words is going to save the situation for you. If it is, and it's a good story from their point of view, and if you have once got their confidence, then there is established magically that cooperation which almost amounts to a conspiracy between storyteller and audience, by which they will be willing to forgive you almost any shortcoming and bear with you through all vicissitudes to the end.

Invention, sympathy, humor, sentiment — all these count, but the one essential thing the writer must have, to succeed at all, is a real and genuine conviction about his subject, whatever it be. It has got to be real to him. He must believe in it himself, or no one else will. He has got to write it out of sheer enjoyment or not at all. This you may say is true of all art, but it is especially true where an audience of children is concerned. They are very ready to detect insincerity, and they will have none of it.

Here at least there must be no Olympic standing outside one's own creation. The personal element counts above all else, and this is a thing that cannot be faked or simulated successfully with all the art and ingenuity at one's disposal. I believe, if one came to analyze it, that all the most successful children's books, irrespective of subject, were actually written in this spirit of sincerity. I am sure that Louisa Alcott's little men and women were as real and living to her as they are to her readers, that she really did enjoy herself whether the public was going to or not. Though she wrote other books later to meet the demand, it is still those earlier ones that one finds thumbed and dog-eared the world over. I think that Ballantyne got just the same thrill over his young icebound adventurers as the boy or girl who is torn from them, with an almost physical shock, by the ringing of the supper bell; that Peter Pan is something far greater than a beautiful and amusing fantasy, and that when Barrie brought Wendy and her brothers back to the open window in obedience to conventional sentiment he felt somehow the same pang of regret that all children do when they watch the play. Edward Lear's extravagances amuse us because they amused him, because he did not merely invent but was himself the man with the Runcible Hat; and the laughter that will echo forever round the Mad Hatter's tea party is only the echo of Lewis Carroll's own mirth in its creation. I don't for an instant believe it is mere artistry alone, however perfect, that moves us when Thumbelina finds the frozen swallow at the end of the mole's tunnel, when the Selfish Giant's garden breaks at last into blossom, or when the trumpets blow so valiantly for Jackanapes on his last ride.

THE STORIES OF HANS ANDERSEN

By Margery Williams Bianco

IT WOULD be interesting to know, supposing certain writers for children of an earlier time were confronted with the general mass of children's literature today, what their impression would be. Of a very considerable expansion, I think, in one sense and a quite marked restriction in another. In an age in which child culture has become a wide and earnest preoccupation there is, side by side with a desire to give the child from the earliest moment every possible opportunity of free development, a definite conspiracy — in fiction at least — to shield him from everything that we consider of an unchildish or non-happy nature. The desire is a quite natural one. The child's life must be gay, must be happy. Open all the windows to the sun, and nothing but the sun. But does it never strike us that in a room filled entirely with sunlight, even sunlight itself may in the end lose its most essential quality?

It is rather a shock to realize that, judged by this standard of imperative cheerfulness, and of what we consider fitted for a child's mind, more than one-half of Hans Andersen's priceless stories might never have passed a publisher's reader. "What?" he might say. "The Fir Tree burn up? Impossible! The little Match Girl can't die; she must be adopted by some really nice family, and the morocco ball should certainly not end in the gutter!"

For nearly all of these stories are sad, and some are more than just sad. Who, for instance, would take the responsibility of including today, in a child's volume, such tales as "Anne Lisbeth," "She Was Good for Nothing," or even "Ib and Christine" or "The Marsh King's Daughter"? It is true that in nearly all modern editions of Andersen there is considerable selection, but in the earlier editions that the children of my generation were brought up on there was no such attempt. At nine years old I remember reading "Anne Lisbeth" as eagerly as "The Little Fir Tree" or "Soup on a Sausage-Peg," and the actual impression that remained was only of a very real and enduring beauty.

In very few of Andersen's stories is there any deliberate effort to choose the bright side of things, or even to ensure a happy ending, unless it occurs naturally. With that he was not in the least concerned, and he was not always concerned with the story itself; many of his best tales are just pictorial impressions. What then is the secret of his appeal to children? I think it is that he was, most essentially, a poet, and that the poet's and the child's mind are a great deal closer than many of us suppose.

He wrote of the world about him and of the things in

it, as colored by his own vision. He didn't choose those things; they were there, and he saw no reason to exclude or disguise them. In this world as he saw it there were drunken old washerwomen, mothers who abandoned their children, dark ruinous houses with neglected and unhappy old people living in them; there were ingratitude, poverty and death, hypocrisy and a great deal of foolish talk, which none than he knew better how to satirize. But there were also faith, charity and humour, love and happy, respected old age; there were enchanted forests, trees that dreamed and birds and beasts who talked, and there was at times, if only for his eyes, a great and shining spiritual light that fell on all these things alike and made one as beautiful as another.

"You must not look at it from the sorrowful side," says the little boy. "To me it all appears remarkably pretty. . . ."

This is not priggishness; still less is it the conventional optimism which, by insisting so much on the "happy ending," also postulates a possible unhappy ending. To Andersen all endings were happy; they were as they should be. Old people die, but would you have them go on living forever? Wicked Inge is punished for her pride, but her soul, after long suffering, turns into the little bird that "flew straight into the sun"; the little Match Girl starved, but she had the vision of eternal life, and the happiest moment of the little Fir Tree is when it bursts into deathless flame.

He had the child mind, which does not conceive of sadness as does the older mind. It is all relative. He was not sorry for this sort of thing at all. What he was really sorry for were the stupid people, the mean and the snobbish and the little-minded, who are blind to beauty though it walks beside them and who can never see life — or death — as the real adventure that it is; the huckster and the Emperor and the Portuguese duck. These he satirizes again and again, but his satire is always kindly; it could not be otherwise.

There has been no writer for children with such amazing range and variety as Andersen. "Tell me a story!" cries the little boy in the "Elder Tree Mother." And the stories begin to come out of the teapot. Each is different from the next; each is as spontaneous as though it were the only story he really wanted to write. He gave of his best unsparingly, and to choose among them were an almost hopeless task.

Everything in his world is animate, has personality and expression; the old street-lamp, the china ornaments, the toys, the poker and the darning-needle, no less than the daisy, the farmyard fowl and the family of snails. This is truly a child's world as a child might conceive it. Everything has its own philosophy, everything moves and acts in its proper way. The soul of the flower is as real as the soul of the poet. The old cupboard creaks; it has a voice and wants to tell us something. Listen, and you will hear the knives and forks chattering in the table drawer. No sooner are the family abed than the tulips and hyacinths jump out of their flowerpots and begin to dance. Everything has a story to tell. And before us, turning those magic pages, there arises surely the most wonderful tapestry that any single human mind has conceived.

I remember a print, seen in childhood, of a well-known poet surrounded by all the creations of his genius. Enormous, indeed, would be the canvas that could contain all the figures to which Hans Andersen gave being and life.

The story of "Waldemar Daa and His Daughters" produces very much the same atmosphere as *Wuthering Heights* or Balzac's *Quest of the Absolute*; against a majestic background of storm and ruin the characters move inexorably to their doom. It has the feeling of some old romantic landscape, blackened with age. Here in a few pages is the tragic story of a whole generation. In "The Marsh King's Daughter," with its rare fantasy and rarer spiritual beauty, is a great conception, but no greater in degree than "Anne Lisbeth," "The Angel" or "The Child in the Grave." Even the humblest things take somehow an element of greatness; he gave nobility to whatever he touched. And if there is one motif that stands out more than any other in his writing, that recurs again and again, it is that expressed most clearly in the words of the angel to the child:

"The good and the beautiful shall not be forgotten; it shall live on in legend and in song."

HITTY: HER FIRST HUNDRED YEARS *

By Rachel Field
Illustrated by Dorothy Lathrop

Reviewed by Margery Bianco

HEN three such persons as Rachel Field, Dorothy Lathrop, and a genuine hundred year old American doll put their heads together, the quite unusual must result. Few books have excited such curiosity as the memoirs of Hitty during their making, and still fewer perhaps have so amply justified all expectations.

I have always contended that the ideal children's book should approach in form as nearly as possible the adult novel. "Hitty" comes close to accomplishing this, and I personally found it far more arresting than the greater number of recent novels I have read. Hitty is a person of much character and originality, and to the reconstruction of her life history, from the Preble homestead in Maine over a hundred years ago to her honored old age in the Eighth Street antique shop, Miss Field has brought not

* New York: The Macmillan Company. 1929.

only the invention, dramatic instinct, and happy use of the unexpected which color all her writing but also an amazing knowledge of certain phases of early American life — as in the description of the whaling voyage — and a feeling for the past which gives extraordinary vitality to her pictures. Children reading *Hitty* will have a clear and very intimate impression of a little girl's life in early New England, of seafaring in the old days, of the Philadelphia Quaker household, of New York in the gay 'seventies, and of the quiet, shuttered existence of the two little gentlewomen in the old New Orleans house.

To read this book is like looking back not only on one's own childhood, but on a long perspective of other childhoods, each picture sharp and clear-cut, like something experienced rather than imagined. Phoebe Preble, the smug meanness of poor Little Thankful, wistful Clarissa, and gay, daring Isabel, all stand before us vividly. They are living children. Each glimpse is admirable. And one of the best scenes of the book is when Sally, that strange, passionate child, who deliberately steals Hitty from the glass case in the Cotton Exposition and secretes her for many weeks, suddenly experiences religion at a negro camp-meeting and, overtaken by judgment in the shape of a thunderstorm, sacrifices her in terrified repentance to the black waters of the Mississippi.

"Oh, God," she wailed, "don't let the lightning strike me dead and all of a heap, don't, please. . . . I tell you I'll give

Hitty back. I won't keep her another minute, Lord — look, here she is! You can have her, only just let me get back to Pa and the *Morning-Glory!*"

She was sobbing hysterically now. I could hear her even above the storm. Now she was running pell-mell down the bank toward the river. I knew only too well what she meant to do with me.

It is rare to find writing like this between the covers of a children's book.

There is humor, tenderness, and a gentle irony in this portrait of the little doll who goes through fire and flood, suffers shipwreck, captivity, and man's ingratitude, whose very existence is at the mercy of those human friends with whose lives, in turn, her own is so closely associated, and who in the end is doomed to outlast them all. "She must be dead a good many years now, even if she lived to be an old lady," remarks Hitty, not without complacency, of little Phoebe Preble.

For like all imaginative writers who find freedom under the covering phrase, "a children's story," Rachel Field has spread her canvas far beyond its acknowledged bounds and created something real, truthful, and enduring — a philosophy of life.

For the pictures by Dorothy Lathrop, who has here given of her very best, only the warmest admiration can be felt. Against a background rich and wise in color, in a hundred expressive poses, she has portrayed Hitty for all time; Hitty prim, composed, with her faint, pleasant smile, whether surrounded by tropic palms and monkeys, floating among the wonders of the rock pool, or falling in all her finery at Mr. Dickens' august feet. Each drawing is a masterpiece. Looking at the serene little face in the daguerreotype frontispiece one feels, with Hitty herself: "What is a mere hundred years to well-seasoned mountain-ash wood?"

As a joint production the book is unsurpassed, nor could its production be bettered.

DE LA MARE

By Margery Bianco

THERE are certain books, poetry especially, which have the power to recall vividly, and after no matter how great a lapse of time, the circumstance of their first reading. They are in the nature of a personal experience, so bound up with a particular moment of life as to become inseparably a part of it.

It was the summer of 1919. The war was newly over, there was a sense of life and the whole world beginning afresh; one could dare to feel gladness without the instant after-tug of fear, and into this time of heightened intensity and awareness came the fresh and poignant beauty of Walter de la Mare's poetry. *The Listeners, Songs of Childhood,* and *Peacock Pie* — those were the three books that make that summer so vivid in memory, and never did three little books fill a summer so completely. We were living in San Remo. Pamela was making those drawings which later — though she had no faintest idea of it then — were to be her part of *Flora*. For five years we had seen little or nothing of the new English books, and it was almost a shock to realize that poems so gay, so tender, so full of lovely and unexpected imagery, existed. They were read again and again till we all but knew them by heart.

Looking back over the years since *Songs of Childhood* and *Peacock Pie* first became widely known, one can only now begin to realize how great has been Walter de la Mare's influence upon the whole field of imaginative literature for children, and the full significance of his contribution. Poetry of and for childhood there had always been, but never poetry like this. He brought not only beauty but something rarer and even more vital, the perception of beauty. His poetry is intensely visual. He is concerned with the living quality of things, their shapes and colors, their texture. When he speaks of a tree, a bird, a flower, it is as though one were seeing it — really seeing it — for the first time, through the eyes of one who is sensitive to beauty in whatever form, even under the guise of what is called ugliness.

To speak of "the eyes of a child" may sound hackneyed and sentimental but that is because most adults have forgotten what that clear and unspoiled vision is really like. A child does see an object clearly because he is looking at it for the first time and he sees it with all the elements

Numbers refer to book list at close of this chapter, showing the volume where story or poem may be found.

of wonder and miracle. De la Mare is among those happy few who can recapture, or perhaps have never wholly lost, the keenness of that vision, which is of the spirit as much as of the physical eye. In "Maria-Fly"[1] he describes the almost unbearable wonder with which a small child looks, for the first time consciously, at a house-fly. Something extraordinary has happened to her; she wants to share, instantly, the wonder that she feels, and all she can explain is that she has just seen a fly, *really* seen it. But no one understands, and in her failure to express just what she means by "seeing" one feels the whole tragic gulf that lies between child and adult.

In *The Memoirs of a Midget*, Miss M., speaking of her childhood, tells how "My eyes dazzled in colors. The smallest of the marvels of flowers and flies and beetles and pebbles, and the radiance that washed over them, would fill me with a mute pent-up rapture almost unendurable." All through the book this sense of visual miracle persists, and we are enthralled by the strangeness, loveliness and sometimes terror of a world seen through almost microscopic eyes.

Beauty and the transience of beauty is the essence of De la Mare's poetry. His cry is always for the grasping, even for a fleeting moment, of that which can never be held.

> Where is beauty?
> Gone, gone:

The cold winds have taken it
    With their faint moan;
The white stars have shaken it,
    Trembling down,
Into the pathless deeps of the sea:
    Cone, gone
Is beauty from me.[2]

And in *Flora*, where a little girl's need to set down on
paper the pictures that grew in her mind moved a great
poet to some of his loveliest and most poignant verse:

One moment take thy rest,
Out of mere nought in space
Beauty moved human breast
To tell in this far face
A dream in noonday seen,
Never to fade or pass:
A breath-time's mute delight:
    A joy in flight:
The aught desire doth mean,
    Sighing, Alas! [3]

Yet never was a poet who has done more to hold that
clear flame of beauty in a shaken world, and never perhaps
has our need of it been more urgent.

Imagination is only another word for the interpretation
of life. It is through imagination that a child makes his
most significant contacts with the world about him, that
he learns tolerance, pity, understanding and the love for

all created things. The generation that has grown up with *Peacock Pie* and *Down-Adown-Derry*, and *Flora*, with all this treasury of wise, gay and lovely verse, has a richer gift than it may know. Poor Miss 7 [2] on her hospital bed, the old grizzled cobbler,[2] Miss Loo[6] and old Susan[6] and flustered Dame Hickory,[5] all the old and tired, the dumb, the foolish and bewildered, become living figures in memory. Many a child afraid of the dark may well go to bed comforted, remembering little Ann [5] in the old house and her wistful, visionary playmate. Lucky are those who still possess *Songs of Childhood* in its original form. Many of the poems from it have been reprinted in *Down-Adown-Derry*, but this particular one, with many others as lovely, is not among them, including "The Pedlar," most haunting of all in sheer beauty.

There have been repeated efforts to draw a line, in imaginative literature, between the child's range and the adult's. Actually no such line exists; children certainly have always disregarded it. It will be a good thing when we cease once and for all to puzzle whether a certain book is "for children" or "about children," and leave the young to choose for themselves. *Crossings* has been spoken of as a touchstone, but it is as much a touchstone for adults as for children — perhaps more. If you do not respond to its magic you have either traveled many leagues from the enchanted land, or will never qualify to enter it. Reality and unreality interpenetrate, but this is confusing only to those who feel that unreality — or that which takes place in the imagination — should be kept always in a properly labeled compartment. For reality is not only a matter of what one can see and touch. It is perhaps this two-world consciousness, a dislike of mental boundaries in any form, which influences de la Mare to leave so many of his stories, in a sense, unfinished. He creates a situation but the explanation of it is left hanging — he has told his tale and it is for the reader, if he cares, to find the key. Often there appears no key, or we seem to grasp at something which at the same time eludes us. Is there any key to "The Almond Tree,"[4] to the story about the grandmother and the children and the chest in the attic,[4] or are there instead a dozen keys of which we are puzzled to take our choice? Can one find any reason except in the writer's artistry for the mounting terror one feels in "Seaton's Aunt"[4] — a tale beside which Henry James' *Turning of the Screw* becomes pallid and artificial. There needs no resort to the supernatural in "Seaton's Aunt." Perhaps her malignity was entirely in Seaton's own mind; perhaps she was no more than an eccentric but really benevolent old lady. Here again the reader must decide for himself.

A great many of de la Mare's tales have this queer under-surface quality of reaching out in unsuspected directions. *The Three Mulla-Mulgars* is something more than a beautiful and moving fantasy; it has dimensions outside the story itself. I think I am right in saying that Walter de la Mare has always had a particular personal affection for this story, more than justified by the delight children take in it and the vividness with which, once read, it remains always in memory. Perhaps he has, too, a special affection for monkeys, of all creatures most intriguing in their near-human quality, for we have the three old apes in "The Isle of Lone,"[5] shambling and pathetic, "bemused by dwarfish wine," and the wonderful story of Jaspar the monkey in *The Lord Fish* — an affection shared by the Chinese. There is, I have heard, an ancient Chinese folk classic, endless like most Chinese folk tales, about the pilgrimage of a monkey in search of the ultimate holiness, which might well have spiritual kinship with the Three Mulla-Mulgars and the valley of Tishnar.

The word "anthology" has always a cold and uninviting sound, rather like "herbarium." It has been left for Walter de la Mare to give us for the first time an anthology which is a living work in itself, not just a collection of poems, thanks to his notes and the introduction in story form which is a key to the whole meaning and function of poetry. *Mr. Nathum's Room* is the starting point from which we must all set out on that journey of the mind which has no ending; it exists not as a point in space, but in spiritual experience. Just as *Come Hither* is in the wider sense an exploration, rather than an anthology, of poetry, so is *Early One Morning* an exploration of childhood, through the gathered fragments of remembered childhood experiences of many times and ages. No more fascinating book about children has ever been written, and none more illuminating.

Behold, This Dreamer, the last of these three anthologies, which seem to have grown inevitably one from the other, gathers the literature of dreams and the dream state, and here again one feels drawn first of all to de la Mare's own personal comments and explorations of the relationship between dreams and imagination, waking life and the unconscious. The introduction is doubly interesting in that so many of de la Mare's tales deal with those curious "extensions of reality" which occur more frequently to the child than to the adult and which the child's mind accepts more readily and without question, so that they seem a natural part of life and only by the later light of acquired reasoning appear in any way strange. Many of us have had at one time or another some such experience, which in retrospect we are contented to class as dream, but who can say where dream ends and reality begins? This is the debatable region to which de la Mare returns again and again, and not the least of his gifts to children is his insistence upon the respect at least, if not understanding, due to the child's imaginative dream-life and its importance to the full growth of the mind. There is no privacy deeper or more precious than that in which the spirit finds its inner nourishment, and it is this that de la Mare defends. In nearly all that he writes there is this reading between the lines, plain for all who may wish to see it, and there are many of his tales which those who think they understand children would do well to consider.

Much has been said, and rightly, in recent years about the need for realism in books for the young, but we must not oppose realism to fantasy, as two necessarily conflicting things. I doubt if any child, nurtured on imaginative tales, was ever seriously handicapped in facing the actual world. It is not fantasy which lulls the mind and deadens the perception of reality, but that form of weak pseudo-realistic writing, too often mistaken for realism, which deliberately falsifies life, through sentimentality, through the desire to portray a world in which everything is easy and simple, all difficulties melt at a touch and reward hangs like a ripe apple for the gathering. The fairy tale is of far sterner metal and the mission of fantasy, far from belying truth, is often to present truth in an understandable form. I am thinking of another great writer and poet, also a crusader like de la Mare, who chose fantasy for the presentation of some of his strongest convictions — G. K. Chesterton. Both are deeply concerned with spiritual truth, both idealists, hating falsity in whatever form, and both are fundamentally fighters in the same cause.

More than ever before we have need, today, of the vital quality of imagination and of poetry and of its power to inspire courage and faith, need of "the music-makers and makers of dreams." We have need of the poet's vision where our own fails, to be reminded that there are qualities and values less perishable than those which shift and crumble around us.

> —beauty vanishes; beauty passes;
> However rare — rare it be;

But there is one beauty which can never vanish, which will endure always, and of this is the poet's gift.

BOOKS BY WALTER DE LA MARE
Mentioned in the preceding paper

[6] *The Listeners, and Other Poems.* 1916. Holt. o.p.

[5] *Songs of Childhood.* 1935. Longmans. o.p. (Little Ann is in "The Phantom").

[2] *Peacock Pie,* A Book of Rhymes. Illustrated by W. Heath Robinson. 1916. Holt.
The Same, illustrated by Claud Lovat Fraser. 1924. Holt.
The Same, with pictures by Jocelyn Crowe. 1936. Holt.
(The verse quoted is from the poem, "The Song of the Secret").

[3] *Flora,* A Book of Drawings. By Pamela Bianco, with Illustrative Poems by Walter de la Mare. 1919. Lippincott. o.p. (The verse quoted is from the poem, "Alas!").

[1] *Broomsticks and Other Tales.* With designs by Bold. 1925. Knopf. (New edition 1942).

The Memoirs of a Midget. 1922. Knopf.

[5] *Down-Adown-Derry,* A Book of Fairy Poems. With illustrations by Dorothy P. Lathrop. 1922. Holt. o.p.

Crossings, A Fairy Play. With music by C. Armstrong Gibbs. Illustrated by Dorothy P. Lathrop. 1923. Knopf. o.p.

[4] *The Riddle* and Other Stories. 1923. Knopf.

The Three Mulla-Mulgars. Illustrated by Dorothy P. Lathrop. 1919. Knopf. (New edition entitled *The Three Royal Monkeys.* Drawings by Mildred E. Eldridge. 1948).

The Lord Fish. Illustrated by Rex Whistler. London. 1936. Faber & Faber.

Come Hither, A Collection of Rhymes and Poems for the Young of All Ages. Embellished by Alec Buckels. 1923. Knopf.

Behold, This Dreamer! Of Reverie, Night, Sleep, Dream, Love-Dreams, Nightmare, Death, the Unconscious, the Imagination, Divination, the Artist, and Kindred Subjects. 1931. Knopf.

Early One Morning in the Spring. Chapters on Childhood as it is revealed in particular in Early Memories and in Early Writings. 1935. Macmillan.

(*Poems for Children.* Selections from *Peacock Pie, Down-Adown-Derry, A Child's Day, Crossings,* and *Flora.* 1930. Holt.

Collected Poems. 1931. Holt. Includes: *Poems, 1906, The Listeners, Motley, The Veil, The Fleeting,* and *Memory.* 1931. Holt. (New edition, 1941).

Poems, 1919 to 1934. 1935. Holt. Supplements *The Collected Poems.*

These collections are included for the convenience of readers looking for poems in books now out of print.)

THE APPLE TREE

By Margery Williams Bianco

N WINTER days the children would put their faces close to the windowpane and say: "If only it were Spring!"

The window looked out on a little garden where in Summer flowers bloomed, but now it was covered with snow. The lilac bushes stood up bare and stiff, and even the wild clematis wore a gray beard like an old man and seemed bowed down with the cold. Only the lame robin, who had stayed behind when all his friends flew southward, would come and hop near the doorsill, ruffling up his feathers, to peck for crumbs, and the tracks of his feet were like tiny hands in the snow.

Then their mother would say: "Cheer up, children! The Winter is nearly over. Very soon Easter will be here, and then we shall have the birds and the flowers back again!"

The little sister asked: "When will it be really Spring? I want it to be Spring now!"

"When Easter comes," said their mother, "then it will be really Spring."

"Does Easter come only in the Spring?" the brother asked.

"Only in the Spring."

"And suppose Easter never came at all!"

"That cannot happen," their mother answered, smiling. "Easter always comes, every year."

So day by day, from the window, the little brother and sister looked out up the road to see if Easter was coming. Nearly all the people who went by they knew by sight, neighbors who would turn their heads and wave a hand to the children as they neared the gate; very few strangers passed by on the road, and none of these looked like Easter.

"Perhaps he will come tomorrow," the brother always said.

"I think he will be dressed all in white," the little sister said, "and wear a shiny thing on his head, like the lady at the circus."

"No," said her brother. "He won't be like that at all. He will ride a big black horse, and he will have a helmet and a golden belt, and carry a sword in his hand."

"I don't want him to have a sword," the little sister said. "I'm afraid of swords!"

"That's only because you're a girl. Swords can't hurt you if you aren't afraid of them." And he began to talk about the kind of horse that Easter would ride, very proud and coal black; it would lift its feet high at every step and have silver bells on the bridle.

II.

The days passed, and presently the snow melted. The sun shone out, and little gray and pink buds showed on the tree branches. Now the lame robin was no longer as tame as he used to be; he came less often for crumbs, and instead was always flitting about the bushes, looking for the best spot to build a nest in when his family came back. The children could play out-of-doors now, but they always kept an eye on the road, in case Easter should pass by when they weren't looking, for it would be dreadful to have waited all these weeks and then miss seeing him. Who knew but he might ride by in the night, and not stop at the cottage at all, especially if he were late and in a hurry? And then one morning their mother stopped in her work to look at the calendar hanging on the wall by the fireplace, and exclaimed: "Why, how quickly the days do go by! Easter will be here before we know it!"

The children looked at each other and smiled.

"You see," the brother said, "He might come any minute now! We must be very careful!"

And so they always played in the front of the house, near the garden gate, where they could watch every one who went past.

One day it really felt like Spring. The sun seemed to shine more brightly than ever before; the sky was blue and the air soft and warm. Even the grass looked greener than usual, and all the new leaves on the lilac bushes had unfolded during the night. In the long grass by the gate there were dandelions in blossom.

"Easter will surely come today!" said the brother. "Let's go a little way up the road, as far as the corner near the dead apple tree, and watch for him there."

So he took the little sister by the hand, and they went out through the gate and on to the road.

"I have saved a piece of bread in my pocket from breakfast," he told her. "So if you get hungry waiting we can sit down on the big stone by the tree and eat."

They set off, the little sister treading very carefully, for she was quite small, and where the path was stony she had to look first and see just where to put down each foot. Here and there along the edge of the road were tiny flowers, blue and white, and these the little sister wanted to stop and gather to give to Easter if they saw him. It took a long time; she gathered them quite short, with hardly any stalk, so that at every few steps they dropped from her hand and had to be picked up again. But the brother was very patient; he waited each time till she was ready to go on again, and in this way they came at last to the corner where the lane joined the highroad.

III.

It was market day in the town, and a number of people were going by on the highway, but they all looked hurried or tired or busy; there was no face among them all that seemed like the face that Easter would have, except one girl, bareheaded, who was singing as she walked. She alone turned her head to smile at the children, but before they could speak to her she had gone on her way.

Nowhere, up or down the road, could they see any one who looked at all like Easter. One man rode by on a horse, but he had no sword, and he looked very cross, so the children were afraid to step out and ask him. But presently a workman came along with a bundle tied to a stick over his shoulder, and he stopped near the bank where the children were sitting to strike a light for his pipe.

"Could you tell me, please," the brother asked him, "whether Easter has gone by yet?"

"Why, no," said the workman slowly, staring at them. "Easter hasn't gone by yet, that I'm sure! I'm just going over to spend Easter Day with my sister now. Over in the town where I've been working the folks don't set much store by Easter, but it's a holiday, so, thinks I, I'll pack up a few cakes for the little ones, and here I am. They'll be looking out for me, surely! I wrote a letter to my sister a week ago, telling her. Just so sure as Easter comes, I said, I'll be there!"

"Then you know what Easter's like?" asked the brother.

"That I do!" said the workman. "Back in the country, when I was a boy, all the folks round about kept Easter, and we made a great feast every year. And that's why I'm going over to my sister's now, for the sake of old times, and to fetch the children a few cakes for the holiday. I'd give you some, and gladly, but it's a big family there and times are hard, so I was able to get only one apicce, all round, but that's better than nothing. Still, I slipped an apple or two in my pocket, coming along, and maybe you'd like them instead."

He pulled two big red apples out of his pocket and gave one to each of them.

"That's better than nothing," he said again as the children thanked him. "And now I must be getting on."

"Perhaps," said the brother, "you'll meet Easter on the road, if he hasn't gone by yet. Do you think you will?"

The workman laughed as if that were a great joke.

"Why, if I don't hurry up," he said, "I surely will! For it's all of twelve miles yet to my sister's house, and I just reckoned to get there by nightfall. So good-by, and a happy Easter to you both!"

He went off up the road, whistling, and walking very fast.

IV.

"Oh, dear," sighed the little sister, "I wish Easter would come quickly! I'm so tired of waiting!"

"We'll wait a little longer," said her brother, "and then we will go back and eat our lunch by the stone under the apple tree." For he too was beginning to feel rather tired of waiting there by the roadside. "You see, if there are so many people who want to keep Easter, that must make it hard for him to get about, and then it isn't his fault that he's late. Perhaps there is some one keeping him now, this very minute, and that's why he hasn't come. Of course, if he has a horse that would make it easier."

He thought of Easter, on a big black horse, riding through the villages, perhaps this very minute, and all the people stretching out their hands to stop him, and wanting him to stay with them. And the black horse tossing his head, to set all the silver bells ringing. It would be a fine thing to travel round with Easter, to walk by his side on the road and hold his horse whenever he dismounted. But the little sister thought of home, and a bowl of bread and milk, for she was getting sleepy.

V.

The road was empty now; for a long while no one had passed up or down. But at last, very far in the distance, they could see some one moving. Under the hot, still rays of the sun, drawing the Spring moisture from the earth, the air seemed to tremble; distant objects, a line of poplar trees, the red-roofed farmhouse by the hill, even the surface of the road, blended and swam together, so that the brother, shading his eyes to gaze up the highway, could not be sure if what he saw were really a figure on a horse and the flash of gold and silver trappings, or just a cloud of dust gilded by the sunlight.

For a moment he thought he heard music, distant trumpets and the shouting of many voices, and then he knew that what he really heard was only the jingle of a sheep-bell in the pasture and the crying of rooks on the plowed field, and that what he saw was no horse and rider, but only some one on foot, coming toward him along the road. And when the figure drew quite near he saw that it was a man, dressed in shabby clothes and walking slowly, as though he had come a long way on foot and was very weary. But when he saw the children he stopped to smile at them and his smile was friendly.

"Are you waiting for some one?" he asked. "For I saw you a long way off, looking out up the road."

"We were waiting for some one," said the brother, "but I'm afraid he can't be coming today; we have waited so long, and I think we will go back now and eat our bread under the tree, for my sister is getting tired."

"I'm tired too," the stranger said, "so if I may I will come with you. Look, your little sister is nearly asleep!"

He picked the little sister up in his arms as he spoke. She was hot and tired and disappointed, and just getting ready to cry, but she put her head down on the man's shoulder and clung round his neck, for he held her like a person who

◄§ 85 §►

is used to carrying little children. So they went, all three of them, back to the turn of the road and down the lane to where the apple tree grew.

VI.

It was quite an old tree, and for many years now it had not borne any blossom. Only a few twisted leaves came on it every Spring, and these soon withered and dropped. It was good to cut down for firewood, the farmer said, but the months passed and no one found the time to cut it, so it had been left standing there. The bare gnarled branches made a good enough shade in the Spring, and just beneath it was a big flat stone, comfortable to sit on, and near the stone a little trickling spring of water.

They sat down, the man with his back against the tree and the boy near him, and the little sister, who had forgotten her tiredness now, sat with her thumb in her mouth and looked at them both.

"I'm sorry I've got only a little piece of bread," said the brother, rather shyly, for he thought that perhaps the man was really a beggar, he was so poorly dressed, and in that case he might be quite hungry. "If I'd known I would have brought more."

"I expect it will be enough for all of us," the man said. And when he took the slice of bread from the brother's hand it certainly did seem larger than one had thought; he broke it into three pieces, and there was quite enough for all of them, as much as they wanted to eat. And it tasted wonderfully good, the brother thought; by far the best bread his mother had ever baked, but perhaps that was because he was so hungry.

They drank from the spring, and the man showed them how to make cups out of leaves, fastened with a thorn, that would hold the water. And after that he told them stories, jolly stories about the little reed that grew down in the ditch and wanted to be an oak tree, and about the king's son who had a dream, and who threw his crown away and went out into the world and became a beggar. He seemed to be a very nice man indeed, and the children were glad they had met him.

VII.

"You must have come a very long way," said the brother presently. For he couldn't help noticing how dusty the man's feet were and that his clothes were quite worn.

"I have come a long way," the man said, "and I have still a long way to go."

"Is your home very far?"

"I have no home," he said. "Sometimes I find friends with whom I can stay for a little while, and they give me shelter. And there are others, good-hearted people, who think they want me; they have business to look after and many things to do, and after a while they find I'm only a trouble to them, and out of place in their households, and they can't spare the time for me, and so I have to go."

"Do you never go back?" asked the brother.

"Yes, if some one dies or there is real trouble in the house and no one else to turn to, then they may remember and send for me, or they just leave the door ajar so I can come in."

"It must be a fine thing to travel all over the world," said the brother. He thought again of Easter and the tall black horse. "Wouldn't it be splendid to be a king, and then you would ride into the city and all the bells would ring and the people come out to meet you!"

But the man didn't answer. Perhaps he hadn't heard or was thinking of something else.

"Did you ever ride on a horse and have a sword?" the brother asked.

"I had a sword once," said the man, "but I gave it away."

"Weren't you sorry afterward?"

But again the man didn't answer; he was murmuring something, looking down at the earth at his feet, and the brother thought: Perhaps he really is sorry about the sword and doesn't like to speak of it. It was something one shouldn't have asked, and he didn't want to hurt the man's feelings. So he said aloud:

"Won't you tell us about some of the fine things you saw when you were traveling?"

The man looked up and smiled at them, and he put his hand inside the torn lining of his coat.

"This," he said, "is the most precious thing that I have found today, and I picked it up by the roadside."

He drew out his hand carefully; something very wonderful must be there, the boy thought, a tiny carved casket, or perhaps a jewel some one had dropped. But when he spread his fingers there was only a little brown bird on his hand, quite dead and limp, with its feathers ruffled, all dusty from lying in the road. The boy was disappointed; it wasn't at all what he expected to see, but the little sister reached out her hand.

"It's a bird!" she cried. "It's a dear little bird, and I don't want it to be dead!"

She stroked it with her tiny finger as it lay on the man's hand, and there were tears in her eyes.

"Don't cry," said the man. "See, we both love the little bird, and I am going to show you something!"

He held the little dead sparrow close to his face while the child watched, and breathed on it; something seemed to stir between his fingers, and when he opened his hand the bird flew away. Straight up in the air it flew, spreading its wings, and as the little sister looked up at it it seemed to change. She thought it had been brown, but now it was snow-white all over, like a white dove, and it hovered a moment above them, and then was gone, far up in the blue sky, but she thought she heard it singing as it flew.

The brother stared. "Where did it go?" he cried. "I saw it lying on your hand and then it wasn't there!"

"It flew away," said the little sister.

"It was dead," said her brother, "and dead things cannot fly."

"I tell you it flew," the little sister repeated. "It flew into the sky, and I saw it!"

And she came near and put her arms round the man's neck and kissed him. "You are a nice man," she said, "and you shall have all the flowers that I gathered for Easter, for you are much nicer than Easter, and no one must ever be unkind to you, because I love you. And I want you to live with us always."

And she looked at him again, and this time she said: "I think you are Easter, for I see a shiny thing on your head."

But though the brother looked, he only saw the sun shining through the branches of the apple tree.

"You are a kind man," he said, "even if you aren't Easter, and some day I hope you will come again and tell us some more stories, for I like your stories very much. And when I grow up and have a sword of my own I am going to give it to you."

VIII.

They went home, and left the man sitting there under the apple tree. His head leaned back against the tree-trunk and his arms were outstretched and he seemed to be sleeping, and in his open hand lay the flowers the little sister had given him. But perhaps he was only resting, for he must have been very tired still.

"I tell you he is Easter," the little sister said. "He is just like I said he would be."

"He isn't Easter," said her brother, "but he is a very nice man, and I am sorry he has to walk so far."

But the little sister pulled at his hand, standing still in the road. "Don't you see?" she cried. "There is something round his head, like gold, and look — the apple tree is all in flower!"

The brother looked.

"It is only the setting sun," he said. "There is no blossom on the tree, for I looked this morning. But tomorrow we'll come back and see."

IX.

In the morning, when the children went back to look, the man had gone. But it was as the little sister had said; the apple tree that had been withered for so many years was in flower.

The boughs, covered with pink-and-white blossoms, stretched out against the blue sky in blessing, and their perfume filled the air all about. It was really Spring; the birds were singing and far away, as the children stood under the apple tree, they could hear the bells ringing for Easter.

The End.

ACKNOWLEDGMENTS

The Horn Book, Incorporated, hereby acknowledges with cordial thanks: The courtesy of William Faulkner and the New York Herald Tribune WEEKLY BOOK REVIEW for permission to quote the two paragraphs on page v. The courtesy of Mr. Seward Collins for permission to reprint in this volume from THE BOOKMAN for November, 1925, the paper by Margery Bianco entitled "Our Youngest Critics." The courtesy of THE SATURDAY REVIEW OF LITERATURE for permission to reprint from the issue of November 16, 1929, Margery Bianco's review of HITTY, HER FIRST HUNDRED YEARS by Rachel Field. Illustrated by Dorothy P. Lathrop. Published by the Macmillan Company. The courtesy of Pamela Bianco for permission to reprint her mother's story THE APPLE TREE, which appeared first in PICTORIAL REVIEW and was published in book form by the George H. Doran Company in 1926.

Margery Bianco's essay "The Stories of Hans Andersen" is reprinted from THE HORN BOOK of May, 1927; that entitled "De la Mare," from THE HORN BOOK for May-June, 1942.

This book is set in Electra, with Deepdene and Weiss Initials used for display, and is printed by the Thomas Todd Company of Boston. The paper is Kilmory Text made by W. C. Hamilton & Sons. Valenti Angelo designed the book and created the designs for the initials and decorations. The book was bound by The Riverside Press, Cambridge.